The House of Fame

The cover shows an eagle, fourth quarter of the thirteenth century (after 1277), tempera colours, pen and ink, gold leaf and gold paint on parchment. The J. Paul Getty Museum, Los Angeles.

Chaucer's

House of Fame

in a

Modern English Verse Translation

by

Simon Webb

More poetry from the Langley Press

Chaucer's Parliament of Fowls

The London Vampires

The Quaker Sonnets

Open House: A Quaker Tale in Verse

A Book of Quaker Poems

Love Sonnets of Dante and His Contemporaries

For free downloads and more from the Langley Press, please visit our website at http://tinyurl.com/lpdirect

Contents

ſi ipſo ſaluator per gratiam
dicit ipſis quem non cogno
uit ſeruiuit mihi· et alte
br· wald non plete meam
z non dilecta mea· dilecta
mea· de illo aut ipſo iude
orum qui magis amaue
rut tenebras quam luce·
dicit deus in pſalmo· ſili

aliem ſtirui ſtir in filij
aliem inuenati ſtir· et
claudicauerut a ſemi
tis ſuis· ethimologia·
nicticorax eſt z ipſa
noctua z eſt auis
luciſuga z ſolem uidere
non patitur· de aquila

aquila talē
hīſe natura·
Eſt ſenuerit
grauantur
ale eius et
obducantur
oculi eius ca
de aquila dicit in
pſalmo centeſimo
ſecdo dauid· Renouabit
tur aquile iuuentus tua
phyſiologus dicit de

ligine· tunc querit fonte
aque z terra ipſm fonte
euolat in altū uſqz ad e
thera ſolis z ibi ſecndit
alas ſuas z gburit cali

Introduction

The name of Geoffrey Chaucer is so closely linked to *The Canterbury Tales*, the title of his masterpiece, that the link is comparable to that between Goethe and *Faust*, and Milton and *Paradise Lost*. But Milton wrote more than *Paradise Lost*, Goethe ventured far beyond the theme of *Faust*, and Chaucer's surviving works encompass rather more than *The Canterbury Tales*. In fact in single-volume editions of Chaucer's works, the *Canterbury Tales* take up rather less than a half of his entire output, if we include the translations and prose pieces. It is certainly splendid to have written a masterpiece, but masterpieces do tend to cast shade on a writer's other works.

The true test of the value of 'an other' work by a great artist is to imagine how that work would stand up if we had no inkling of that artist's masterpiece or masterpieces. This involves the critic in the painful business of trying to imagine the world without *Faust*, *Paradise Lost*, *The Canterbury Tales*, etc., but it can be an illuminating thought-experiment. This technique, applied to Chaucer's *House of Fame*, brings a neglected masterpiece out of its deep shadow and allows us to appreciate how highly developed Chaucer already was as a poet when he began *The House of*

Fame, a composition of which is thought to pre-date the *Canterbury Tales* by some years.

Here, in a poem where Chaucer himself appears as a character, we already have his engaging, disarming pose as an ignorant, lovelorn idiot, a man devoted to Venus who has, however, never enjoyed any benefit from his devotion; who tells us he has no mastery of verse, and calls on Apollo and various other deities to help him to at least set down his thoughts in a readable form.

Part of Chaucer's pose of uselessness and unworthiness in *The House of Fame* is to do with the medieval tradition of courtly love; the bizarre, ritualised and theoretically platonic love that underpinned many of the great literary works of the Middle Ages. According to the rules of courtly love, a man loved a woman in a hopeless, servile way, with (in theory) no hope of reward or even recognition. He would try to appeal to the object of his affections (or just try to grab her attention) with extravagant gifts and acts of devotion. He would slavishly follow her every whim and beg for any slight token of her regard, such as a glove of hers to wear in his hat. It is implied in *The House of Fame* that Chaucer doesn't even have a mistress of this type – he is merely devoted to Venus, the goddess of love. He claims something similar in his poem *The Parliament of Fowls.*

The poet's familiar attempts to make himself seem pathetic receive an extra fillip in *The House of Fame* because here we see him as a hapless traveller in the land of dreams, trapped in the claws of a giant golden eagle which carries him up and up through the vast spaces of the medieval conception of the cosmos. Here, where earth can only be seen as a tiny pin-point,

Chaucer is sweating with fear and completely helpless, and seems like a pin-point himself.

Chaucer's inclusion of himself in *The House of Fame* will be familiar to readers of *The Canterbury Tales* and other works. In *The House of Fame* we get a snap-shot of Chaucer's daily life, as described to him by the garrulous eagle:

> . . . after all
> Your day-job work, your reckonings and sums,
> Instead of rest and entertainment, you
> Just go straight home, and, dumb as any stone
> You sit and read the umpteenth book and look
> As dazed and pale as any eremite:
> Although you don't embrace his abstinence . . .

At this time, the poet was working as comptroller of customs for the port of London, an extremely important job, and was living above the actual gate called Aldgate in London. According to the eagle, Chaucer's leisure time consisted of nothing but reading, which is why Jupiter the king of the gods, who is the eagle's master, has detailed the bird to snatch up the poet's dreaming self and show him some curiosities of the cosmos, to broaden his mind.

The ignorance Chaucer affects is contradicted throughout the poem by his many learned references to earlier literature. These include everything from ancient Greek philosophy (Plato and Aristotle) to Latin classics such as Virgil's *Aeneid*, and writers nearer to Chaucer's own time, such as Dante.

Chaucer manages to wear his learning lightly not only by maintaining his doltish pose, but by interspersing literary references with mind-boggling action and lively conversation, the latter usually shared by himself and the golden eagle.

Although the eagle is a powerful symbol, and an important source of information about where Chaucer is and what is happening to him, he is also a realistic and well-rounded character. The bird has no tendency to play down his own learning, being excessively proud of it, and eager to expend it on the helpless Chaucer, his passenger and captive audience. He not only explains everything at length – he even repeats himself, and near the end of their time together he asks Chaucer how he did as a guide. At one point the usually polite Chaucer becomes exasperated and tries to put the eagle off saying any more:

The eagle cried, 'You're fantasising now,
When really you should listen to your guide:
Myself, who's ready to describe to you
The stars, unless you say you know them all?'
'Oh no, I can't learn anything,' I said
'About the stars: I fear I am too old.'
'A shame,' the eagle said, 'I'd planned to teach
You all their names and all the star-signs' names,
And where they are: I think that you should learn
Their places in the heavens, because when
You read in poems of how ancient gods
Turned birds or fish or beasts into bright stars,
Such as the Bear or Raven, or the harp
Of Arion, Castor, Pollux, Delphinus,
The Pleiades, or Atlas' seven girls,
You'll know their names, and how they came to be.'
'Please don't,' I cried, 'I just don't need to know
All this, I'll trust the books I have that treat
Of this to keep me in the know . . .

Chaucer's own speech as reported in *The House of Fame* is informal, littered with typical fourteenth-century oaths, direct and powered by his emotions. His feelings as depicted in the poem include puzzlement, outright sweaty fear, amazement, and his typical feeling of unworthiness, in this case either to experience the dream or to write a poem about it. In his depiction of his own emotions, Chaucer follows Dante, whose own feelings during his journey through hell, purgatory and heaven are such an important aspect of his *Divine Comedy*.

The poet's depiction of himself as a cowardly fool, his interaction with the garrulous eagle, his own down-home utterances and his wry comments on the events he recounts all add to the humour of *The House of Fame*, which the poet originally wrote in octosyllabic couplets, which somehow always seem to suggest comedy in English. Here is Chaucer's version of the first passage of my translation printed above:

For when thy labour doon al ys,
And hast mad alle thy rekenynges,
In stede of reste and newe thynges
Thou goost hom to thy hous anoon,
And, also domb as any stoon,
Thou sittest at another book
Tyl fully daswed ys thy look;
And lyvest thus as an heremyte,
Although thyn abstynence ys lyte.

The octosyllabic couplet is two crucial syllables short of the ten syllables of the heroic couplet, a line Chaucer uses with great effect in his *Canterbury Tales*.

The heroic couplet was also the line of choice for Dryden and Pope, and the unrhymed iambic pentameter, called blank verse, was Shakespeare's worthy vehicle. For the purposes of this discussion, blank verse comprises heroic couplets shorn of their rhymes.

As well as suggesting lightness, comedy and a certain primitive crudeness, which may detract from their capacity to carry serious matter, octosyllabic couplets also demand a new rhyme from the poet every five to seven words, on average. This is rather fewer than the nine or so words between rhymes in the heroic couplet, and can seem like a bit of a straitjacket, especially if the poet is tackling something long. It is possible that Chaucer failed to finish *The House of Fame* because he grew weary of the form to which he had committed himself. Near the end of the poem, he even admits that he has something he could tell us, but frankly can't be bothered to do so. He says that other writers might attempt it, and that in any case it is bound to come out sooner or later:

. . . And as I roamed about and tried to learn
The nature of this house, and tried to trace
The truth of something I had vaguely heard
About some country there (I will not say
Exactly what it was – there is no need,
And other writers can relate the thing;
The truth will out though soon or late, as sheaves
Of wheat must leave the barn or go to waste) . . .

Octosyllabic lines are a feature of the verse form Chaucer uses for *The Tale of Sir Thopas*, the first tale Chaucer himself tries to tell to his fellow pilgrims in *The Canterbury Tales*. The poet is not allowed to finish this knightly tale because he is interrupted by Harry Bailly, the landlord of the Tabard Inn at Southwark where the pilgrimage had begun. Bailey had decided to join Chaucer and the other pilgrims on their trip to Canterbury, and appointed himself master of ceremonies with command of their scheme to tell each other stories along the way. Bailly breaks into *Sir Thopas* when he becomes too exasperated to hear any more:

"Namoore of this, for Goddes dignitee,"
Quod oure Hooste, "for thou makest me
So wery of thy verray lewednesse,
That also wisly God my soule blesse,
Min eres aken of thy drasty speche.
Now swich a rym the devel I biteche!
This may wel be rym dogerel," quod he.

The host goes on to say that Chaucer's verse is 'not worth a turd', and his interruption marks a return to heroic couplets. The *Tale of Melibee*, which Chaucer goes on to tell, is in prose. Can the rejection of *Sir Thopas* in *The Canterbury Tales* be a reflection of Chaucer's growing impatience with this type of verse? Could the text of *Sir Thopas* be the remains of another short-lined poem Chaucer did not finish?

Like *The Parliament of Fowls*, *The Book of the Duchess* and *The Legend of Good Women*, Chaucer's *House of Fame* is a 'love-vision', a type of narrative poem popular in medieval times, which recounts a dream where the dreamer learns something important about love. The type of love that is meant here is the aforementioned courtly love.

In the unfinished *House of Fame*, Chaucer spends so many lines telling us about his conversation with the eagle, how he got to the House, and how Fame herself, the owner of the House, operates, that the poem breaks off after over two thousand lines without the love-lesson as such actually emerging. The elements of *The House of Fame* that make love an important theme of what we have of the poem are the frequent mentions of Venus, a goddess to whom Chaucer professes himself devoted, and the inclusion of famous lovers, particularly women who have been betrayed in love by men. Pride of place among these is Dido, the queen of Carthage who was seduced and deserted by Aeneas, the wandering prince of Troy.

Dido is a good example of how love and fame are intertwined because in Virgil's *Aeneid*, which is Chaucer's main source for her story, fame is such an important element in the epic that it can be counted as another character. Indeed, with reference to Dido, Virgil uses a personification of Fame as the means by which news of the African queen's shameful seduction is spread. Virgil also uses a few lines to describe Fame's nature and origins. This part of Book IV of the *Aeneid* was an important source for Chaucer's own description of Fame in *The House of Fame*:

Fame, the great ill, from small beginnings grows:
Swift from the first; and ev'ry moment brings
New vigour to her flights, new pinions to her wings.
Soon grows the pigmy to gigantic size;
Her feet on earth, her forehead in the skies.
Inrag'd against the gods, revengeful Earth
Produc'd her last of the Titanian birth.

14

Swift is her walk, more swift her winged haste:
A monstrous phantom, horrible and vast.
As many plumes as raise her lofty flight,
So many piercing eyes inlarge her sight;
Millions of opening mouths to Fame belong,
And ev'ry mouth is furnish'd with a tongue,
And round with list'ning ears the flying plague is hung.
She fills the peaceful universe with cries;
No slumbers ever close her wakeful eyes;
By day, from lofty tow'rs her head she shews,
And spreads thro' trembling crowds disastrous news;
With court informers haunts, and royal spies;
Things done relates, not done she feigns, and mingles truth
with lies.
Talk is her business, and her chief delight
To tell of prodigies and cause affright.

(from Book IV of Dryden's translation)

While Chaucer draws on Virgil for Fame herself, he
turns to Ovid for Fame's House:

There is a spot convenient in the centre of the world,
between the land and sea and the wide heavens, the meeting
of the threefold universe. From there is seen all things that
anywhere exist, although in distant regions far; and there all
sounds of earth and space are heard. Fame is possessor of
this chosen place, and has her habitation in a tower, which
aids her view from that exalted height. And she has fixed
there numerous avenues, and openings, a thousand, to her
tower, and no gates with closed entrance, for the house is
open, night and day, of sounding brass, re-echoing the tones
of every voice. It must repeat whatever it may hear; and

15

there's no rest, and silence in no part. There is no clamour; but the murmuring sound of subdued voices, such as may arise from waves of a far sea, which one may hear who listens at a distance; or the sound which ends a thunderclap, when Jupiter has clashed black clouds together. Fickle crowds are always in that hall, that come and go, and myriad rumours—false tales mixed with true—are circulated in confusing words. Some fill their empty ears with all this talk, and some spread elsewhere all that's told to them. The volume of wild fiction grows apace, and each narrator adds to what he hears. Credulity is there and rash Mistake, and empty Joy, and coward Fear alarmed by quick Sedition, and soft Whisper—all of doubtful life. Fame sees what things are done in heaven and on the sea, and on the earth. She spies all things in the wide universe.

(from Book XII of Ovid's *Metamorphoses*, translated by Brookes More)

Chaucer's treatment of both Fame and her House are so similar to those of the Latin poets Ovid and Virgil that modern readers might be tempted to accuse him of plagiarism, and even a lack of imagination. This would be to misunderstand the role of the poet in medieval Europe. Originality and inspiration were little regarded in those days: tradition, book-learning and knowledge were more highly valued, not least because in a world where the vast majority of people were illiterate, books and learning were comparatively rare. There was also a sense, in Chaucer's time, that English was being rediscovered as a literary language in England, after many years when French and Latin held the field. Part of Chaucer's role, as both author and translator, was to put old stories written in other languages, whether dead or alive, into English. The medieval reliance on old learning – the old fields from which, in a phrase from *The Parliament of Fowls*, new corn could spring, was pretty disastrous for medieval medicine, but the guidance of such past masters as Virgil and Ovid could not but help Middle English literature.

Although *The House of Fame* is partly derived from ancient sources, and tells us a great deal about the mind-set of the medieval *literati*, it has some ideas that are still very relevant to us today. Although Venus and love are important presences in the poem, the titan Fame is central to the story, as she is to much of modern culture. She was and is a treacherous, unreliable creature, a valuable ally who can quickly become a dangerous enemy, and her judgements (if we can call them that) are disturbingly arbitrary. Modern people who want to live obscurely find themselves 'backing into the spotlight' like the British World War II hero T.E. Lawrence; people who want to be famous for one thing become well-known for another; and people who actively court fame remain unknown, or are only famous for the proverbial fifteen minutes.

As the reader may already have gathered from my discussion of Chaucer's metre, I am an enthusiast for blank verse, the metre into which I have previously translated *The Parliament of Fowls*. Although a translation of Chaucer's *House of Fame* into octosyllabic couplets was successfully brought off by Brian Stone for Penguin in the nineteen-seventies, I thought that in the case of *The House of Fame* a complete change of metre might allow for more flexibility and readability, and bring out different aspects of the original. I have been encouraged in this by recent successful attempts by other writers to translate, for instance, Dante and Virgil into English

17

blank verse.

I have heeded warnings from another Dante, Dante Gabriel Rossetti, about the dangers of putting footnotes into pages of verse and, as in my version of *The Parliament of Fowls*, have limited explanatory notes to a glossary. Because of the nature of Chaucer's poem, the words explained by these notes are all the names of persons (including gods, goddesses, etc.) and places.

Book I

Reader, may God bless every dream you have,
And make it good: I wonder, by the rood
What causes dreams: I fear my paltry wit
Just cannot grasp it – some dreams come by day
And some by night; some prophesy, some don't,
Some offer revelations, while some dreams
Bring visions: some are *dreams* and some are *swoons*,
And no one ever seems to dream the same.
Some dreams are phantoms, some are oracles,
But why? Don't ask me – ask someone who knows
About these miracles; let him explain,
As I cannot, and never hope to know
The answer, even if I worked away
At what dreams mean, how long they last, and all
Their varied types and causes; whether some
Have more than one cause; whether different types
Of people meet with different types of dreams,
Or if a dreamer who is abstinent
Or sick, or desperate, or locked away
In some unhealthy prison, or removed
From everything he knows, or over-stuffed
With curious studies or with misery
(So that his life seems hopeless and his dread
Of everything puts him beyond all help)
Or if devoted prayers and holy thoughts

Cause some to dream, or if the cruel life
That lovers lead, so full of hope and fear,
Engenders visions, or if spirits come
At night and force us to dream as they will,
Or if the perfect human soul itself
Can see into the future and predict
By sights and symbols all that may befall
The dreamer (but our wit can't always grasp
The true interpretation of the sights
The true soul sends to warn our sleeping selves) -
All this is quite beyond me – go and read
What scholars say about these things: I won't
Presume upon the reader with my thoughts:
I'll only pray to God for pleasant dreams,
And swear that no one ever had a dream
As wonderful as I dreamed on the tenth
Of last December; which I'll now describe.
But first, I must invoke the God of Sleep
And show him my devotion, so that he
Will help me with my task. They say he lives
Upon the very fringe of the great world
In far Cimmeria, by Lethe's stream
(A noisome water-way from Hell) and there
He sleeps eternally inside a cave
With all his thousand sons: this Morpheus
I now invoke, as master of men's dreams.
And also I invoke another God,
That is, and was, and ever shall be Lord,
The *primum mobile* of everything,
In hopes that He will give my hearers joy
In all their dreams this year, and let them stand
Warm in the soft approval of their loves,
Or else wherever they would rather stand,
And shield them all from poverty and shame,
And from bad luck and rotten health as well,

And send them everything that they might want,
And send them also the ability
To like my little poem, and not spot
Its many grievous faults: clear all their minds
Of envious malice – if they feel they must
Cast shade on it and bring their scorn to bear
To run it down like villains – Jesus God
Please punish them with every plague that can
Alight on humans; though they dream bare-foot
Or in their shoes – make them deserve their fate
As Croesus did, the King of Lydia
Who died high on a gibbet when he failed
To understand a dream – thus critics should
All meet their end – that is my gift to them!
But listen: I must now recount to you
What happened in my dream before I woke.
December tenth it was, as I have said,
When I lay down to sleep as usual.
I quickly fell asleep, as if I'd walked
A pilgrimage to good St Leonard's shrine
That stretched two miles or more – I was that fagged.
Now as I slept I dreamed I was inside
A temple made of glass: within this place
Were more fine statues made of gleaming gold
Standing on plinths, and more stone pinnacles,
And more fine curious portraits, and more shrines,
And more old cunning carvings than I'd seen
In all my life. I knew not where I was,
But thought the place belonged to Venus when
I saw a painting of the goddess there
All naked in the sea: there was her crown
Of roses, red and white, and her fine comb,
Her doves, and Cupid also – her blind son,
And brown-faced Vulcan. As I walked around
I found a wall of brass, and read on it

The words, 'Now I will try my best to sing
The story of a man and of his arms:
The man forced to escape from burning Troy
By destiny, who wandered long in pain
Until he reached the shore of Italy.'
Thus it began, and I will write some more
Of what it said: I saw the fall of Troy,
Brought down by nothing but old Sinon's lies:
He was the smooth-faced Greek who cunningly
Persuaded them to drag the wooden horse
Inside the gates of Troy; a deadly gift.
And after this I saw the tale went on:
How Troy's tall towers were sacked and quite destroyed,
King Priam slain, Polytes his son too
By ruthless Pyrrhus, and his castle burned.
At sight of this fair Venus came to earth
And warned Aeneas to escape the town,
And so he did: Anchises, Venus' love,
Aeneas' father, clung to his son's back.
Anchises in his turn saved from the flames
His household gods: Aeneas could not save
His wife Creusa, though she followed them
With Iulo and Ascanius, her sons.
Their flight lay through a forest, and by chance
The trio lost their way – Creusa died
Though how, I do not know, and when her love
The brave Aeneus went to search for them,
He found Creusa's ghost, who said to him
That he must leave his search and flee the Greeks
And go to Italy: such was his fate.
Oh, I was sad to see Aeneus' wife
Appearing as a ghost to speak to him,
And tell him he should guard their handsome son.
There I saw graven on the wall the tale

22

Of how Aeneas and his father and
Their followers all took to ships and made
For Italy directly as they could;
But then cruel Juno, Jove's own wife, stepped in
And thwarted them because she hated Troy.
She ran to Aeolus, the god of winds,
And madly screamed at him that he should blow
So hard upon the Trojan fleet that they
Would all be drowned – the women, children, all.
And then upon the wall I saw a storm
So furious that any heart would ache
To see it there, depicted on the wall.
But then I noticed Venus, mistress mine,
Weeping and pleading with the mighty Jove
To save the Trojan navy and her son
Aeneas: then she gave great Jove a kiss
And for this kiss the Thunderer restrained
The tempest, saved the Trojans, who arrived
At length upon the Carthaginian coast.
The morning after they had secretly
Arrived upon that coast a Trojan knight,
By name Achates, and the brave Aeneas
Met with what seemed to be a huntress there,
Whose hair was loose and blowing in the wind.
It was Aeneas' mother in disguise,
And he began to tell her the sad tale
Of all the ships that he had lost at sea
In the great storm, and how he didn't know
Where all the Trojans in them might be now.
Fair Venus tried to comfort him and said
That he should go to Carthage, where he'd find
All of the friends he'd lost when their sad fleet
Had broken up and scattered in the sea.
Thanks to his mother Venus, Aeneas
Found favour with Queen Dido, who was queen

Of Carthage, and to summarise, she soon
Allowed the Trojan every liberty
A husband would enjoy, except that they
Were never married. I will not recount
In too great detail everything love gave
To this grand couple; anyway this 'love'
Is something I don't know about at all.
I'll skip the story of their growing love,
And say what I saw next upon the wall.
I saw the Trojan hero telling her
The details of his scrapes upon the sea,
And saw how she believed him, and then how
Her heart was quickly won and lost to him
Whom she declared her love, her lust, her life,
And made him her one lord, and gave him all
That any woman could yield to a man.
His sea-tale had convinced her that he was
The best man that had ever lived, but he
Betrayed her and she slew herself – which shows
How looks can hoodwink us and an unknown
Suitor can do great harm if he prevails.
By Christ, the moral of this story is
That everything that glitters is not gold,
And looks can cover multitudes of sins.
So heed the moral, Everywoman! Don't
Embrace a man because he's beautiful,
Or speaks well, or is charming – look behind
The fine facade that captivates the eye
And see the natural man who stalks his prey
And having got her, casts her off again,
Finding some cause why she is not quite right:
She's false, she's secretive, she is unkind.
All this I find in Dido's tragedy
Who loved a guest too soon: now I'll apply
A true old proverb: look at the herb well

24

Before you put it to your ailing eye.
So this was brave Aeneas: he betrayed
His hostess, and when she could see the scope
Of his betrayal: utter, ruthless, cold,
And that he would embark and sail north-west
To meet his destiny in Italy,
She wrung her hands and cried 'Woe' and 'Alas!
Are all men like this? Are they never true?
Will they not ever stay with just one love,
But look for three instead? One for her fame,
To make his name resound down through the years,
And one for friendship, number three for fun,
Or maybe for her money?' Thus the queen
Complained, as I saw graven in my dream
Upon the wall: I have no other source.
'Alas!' she cried, 'my lover, pity me,
You kill me if you leave me, Trojan, stay!
Have pity on your Dido, Aeneas!
Will you forget the pledges that you made?
Will not my love still hold you here, cruel man?
Or do you mean to kill me? Pity me
If any man had pity on his love!
Oh, now I see that women have no art
To find the mind's construction in the face,
And now I see that every woman is
Served just like this at least once in her life:
All men know this, but women, not so much!
Your love lasts for a season, but soon ends:
You leave us shattered – reputation, pride,
Are both thrown down: I know I will be sung
And read about and laughed at endlessly
In Carthage and through Africa – oh Fame!
How swift you are, and wicked! Everything
Is known to you, though covered with a mist
At first, and when my plight is known, my name

Will last in infamy eternally,
And nobody will blame Aeneas, but
Will say that I continued in my lust
After the Trojan fleet had gone away:
That is the reputation I have now!'
The die was cast, and Dido never could
Undo what she had done: her pining speech
Was not a remedy, and when she knew
The Trojans had all gone down to their ships,
She went back to her chamber and she called
Her sister Anne, and said she had approved
Her love for the fine Trojan; then she split
Her own heart with a knife, and killed herself.
If you would like to read more of her tale,
Then turn to Virgil's *Aeneid*, or find
The letter of complaint that Dido wrote
To cruel Aeneas among Ovid's works:
In full, the story is too long for me
To set down here, though God knows I would like
To show you how a lie can do such harm,
Though many other books have touched this theme
And every day new instances are shown
Of lying lovers; like Demophoon
Who married Phillis, but deserted her
Although she was a fair princess of Thrace
And so she hanged herself when she despaired
Of his return, and knew that he had lied:
A dreadful story, made to break your heart!
And there are others: think of Briseis,
The widow cold Achilles turned away;
Oenone, lying Paris's first wife,
Hypsipyle, Medea, Jason's wives,
Iole, who distracted Hercules
From Deianira, and caused the hero's death.
And I could also mention Theseus

(I'd throw him to the devil, if I could)
Who left his Ariadne even though
She helped him to avoid becoming meat
To feed the Minotaur. She pitied him
And saved him, but he never pitied her,
And later left her sleeping all alone
On Naxos, a bare island: he sailed off
Together with her sister Phaedra, though
He'd sworn to marry Ariadne who
Had saved his life: he'd sworn by everything
A man can swear by, but deserted her,
Although the Cretan girl thought Theseus
Was everything she valued in the world:
At least, that's what my sources say of her.
(There's two sides to each story, so they say,
And so in fairness to Aeneas' name
I should recount that Mercury, the god
Of messages was sent to Africa
To tell the Trojan to give up that place
And leave his mistress and her new-built town.)
The carvings in the temple then revealed
How all the Trojans sailed to Italy,
And how a fearful tempest battered them,
And how Aeneas' steersman fell asleep
And tumbled from his post into the sea.
The temple walls recounted how Aeneas
Then begged the Sibyl to assist him with
A visit to the underworld to see
His father, old Anchises, where he found
Together with his father many more
Pale shades: his steersman Palinurus and
The Trojan's mistress Dido, freshly dead,
Deiphobus his brother – there they were:
Familiar faces trapped for evermore
Amid the torments of the nether world.

27

(To read about the pains of hell you must
Refer to Dante, Virgil, Claudian.)
And then I saw, all set out on the wall
Aeneas set his foot upon the shore
Of Italy, and make a treaty there
With King Latinus, but he had to march
To many battles to assert his rights,
And kill King Turnus, wed Lavinia
And read the runes the gods set out for him.
Thus did Aeneas triumph, though the wife
Of Jove, resentful Juno, worked against
His efforts, using all her dreadful power
To bring him down: but Jupiter stepped in
And helped him against Juno, because he,
The Thunderer, remembered Venus' kiss:
Oh Venus, help us all this self-same way
And lighten all our sorrows if you can!
When I had looked in every corner of
Fair Aphrodite's temple, I declared
'Oh Lord who made us, never have I seen
Such noble images or sumptuous scenes
As I have studied on this church's walls;
But who the artist was, or artists were
Or even where I am, I've no idea!
What country is this, even? I must go
Out by the gate, and look around to see
If anyone can clue me in on this.'
Outside, I saw a barren land that stretched
As far as I could see: no tree or bush
Grew there, there was no little town to see
Or even any houses: even grass
Was missing; only dusty desert sand
As fine as you might find in Libya
Was there, and not a single creature stirred.
'Oh Christ,' I thought, 'who lives in heaven above,

Save me from phantoms and illusions,'
And as I said this, I cast up my eyes
To heaven in pure devotion, where I saw
To my surprise, high up beside the sun,
As high as I could stretch my widening eyes,
A bird, a golden eagle, soaring there.
As true as death, who waits for all of us,
This eagle was much bigger than the birds
Of his prestigious species that I'd seen,
In real life, when I wasn't in a dream,
And his gold plumage gleamed in such a way
It seemed that mother nature had produced
Another sun; but this one of pure gold.
And this strange bird was flying down to me.

Book II

Now listen, all who know our English tongue
And you shall hear described a noble dream,
Far finer than the dreams of Scipio,
Or Turnus, or Isaiah, or Pharaoh,
Nabuco, or the dream of Elcanor!
Oh Cipris, fair and blissful, condescend
To help me tell this vision properly;
And muses on Parnassus, by the well
Of Helicon, assist me in my task;
And Thought, who put this vision in my head,
Make good your reputation and work hard
To free it from the store-house of my brain;
Unless you'd rather people didn't know
The details of this very curious dream.
The golden eagle with his gleaming wings
That I have mentioned, soared about the sky,
And I observed him more and more, but there
Was not a hint of thunder in the blue,
Or lightning that can strike a mighty tower
And turn it all to powder. The great fowl
Swept down like lightning when it chanced to see
Your author roaming in the desert there.
He swooped, and grabbed me in his mighty claws
Equipped with fearful nails, and soared aloft

Again, but this time lightly carrying
Yours truly, dangling like a captured lark.
How high we soared, I really cannot say:
In truth I was astonished, and my mind
Was emptied out by panic – his wing-strokes,
Our growing height, my fear, all made me numb.
I dangled in his claws a long, long time,
Before the eagle opened up his beak
And cried, 'Wake up!' but in a voice I knew,
Although I could not place it at that time.
The speech of the gold eagle rallied me:
He spoke so well, I found it comforting.
I came back to myself, and his warm claws
Restored my body's warmth, and my chilled heart
Began to beat again: the bird began
To cheer me up with further warming words,
And said, 'By good Saint Mary you are hard
To carry, though you needn't be at all.
The wise God helps my labours, and no ill
Will come to you by this, but rather good:
This whole thing is designed to help you learn;
So open up your eyes and look around!
I am your friend, and cannot do you harm.'
But I was not assured – I thought that God
Who made us all, had chosen this strange way
For me to die; or maybe Jove now planned
To lift me up and turn me to a star.
What else could all this mean, I thought, I'm not
Young Ganymede, or Enoch, or Elias
Or Romulus, who all were lifted up
To heaven by Jove: this Ganymede I'd read
Became his butler – that was what I thought,
But he that bore me seemed to read my thoughts,
And said, 'You're wrong – the great god Jupiter
Is nowhere hereabout, I'll tell you that,

And nobody will turn you to a star!
But I will tell you what we are about
Before we go much further – what I am
And where we two are going I'll reveal,
And why I came to fetch you from the sand:
All this I will explain, in hopes that you
Will cease your trembling now, and lose your fear.'
'Please do,' I cried, and 'Good' the eagle said.
'The eagle who now holds you in his feet
And makes you tremble to your very bones
Lives with great Jove, the mighty Thunderer
Who orders me to fly great distances
On his great errands – you are one of those.
I tell you truthfully, he pities you
Because you serve blind Cupid, his nephew
And also Venus, though without reward
As yet, and you have used your feeble wit
To write out ditties, songs and even books
In rhyme and rhythm to the god of love
To celebrate his servants, and the folk
Who hope to join his service, though yourself
The busy writer have had none of it.
Now, Jove has noticed how you sit all night
And make your head ache humbly setting down
Your praises of his art, to you unknown
Except by study; how you further his
Great cause and those of all his followers,
And praise and honour him and them and don't
Cast shade on any of the ways of love,
Although you dance among the sorry rout
Of those whom love has not advanced – till now.
My master, Jupiter, has seen the ways
You help out love, but also he perceives
How ignorant you are of love's glad news:
Not only news of love from far away

But even love among your neighbours, who
Might duel against each other at your door
But you don't see or hear them. After all
Your day-job work, your reckonings and sums,
Instead of rest and entertainment you
Just go straight home, and, dumb as any stone
You sit and read the umpteenth book and look
As dazed and pale as any eremite,
Although you don't embrace his abstinence.
And therefore Jove has detailed me to take
Love's scribbler through the sky and let him see
The curious place we call the House of Fame,
To entertain you and inform your thought
And recompense you for your labour spent
For reckless Cupid, without hope of thanks.
And so at last, the god of love consents
That you should be rewarded in some way,
And that is why you're here – and your reward
Will be to see such sights and hear such things
Concerning love, that they will cheer you up.
The menu will include some wise old saws
Concerning love, and also cunning lies;
New loves, and loves requited at long last,
And loves that blossom against common sense,
Like blind men hunting after hares, and loves
Which nobody can credit; love that seems
As true as steel, and brings much happiness,
And love that brings discord and jealousy;
Gossip and murmuring and shocking news,
And arguments repaired with sticky lies.
You'll see more beards neglected through despair,
Left innocent of scissors, in two hours
Than grains of sand upon a beach; you'll see
More holding hands and more re-kindled loves
Between forgotten friends, more fond accords

Than chords in music, and more days of love
And true loves pledged than all the grains of corn
That may be found on farms throughout the land:
I hope you credit what I've said to you?'
'I don't,' I answered him, 'so help me God!'
'And why not?' asked the eagle. 'Because I,'
I said, 'cannot believe that all the news
Of love in all the realm can ever be
Collected in the way that you imply;
No, not if all the magpies in the land,
And all the human spies should listen out
Like agents in the pay of fickle Fame
For news of love; how can they hear all this?'
'They can, I can assure you,' said the bird,
'And if you listen, I will tell you how,
But listen carefully and understand.
And first, I will explain where Fame resides,
Though you know this already – you have read
The details in your Ovid, but I'll still
Tell you her palace stands right in the midst
Of heaven, earth and sea, so any word
That's said in any one of these three zones
Will get here, though it's spoken secretly
Or openly, or whispered, read or sung,
In fear or confidence: it must come here
From any tongue, there is no other way.
And how? Why, Geoffrey, I will try to show
How this can happen, with all clarity.
You know, I'm sure, that every kind of thing
Belongs in some one place where it can thrive
And also can survive the best; thus stones
And lead, and anything of weight must fall
If you should drop them: fire, and smoke, and sounds
Are light, and thus they fly into the air,
If they can get to it – up they will go

So light things rise, and heavy things must fall.
Thus rivers, by their nature, cannot help
But run into the sea, where fish must live,
Or else in other waters, and the trees
Can only thrive in earth: thus everything
Has its own mansion, where it needs much lodge,
To which it must return or come to bad.
Now this is widely understood: Plato
And Aristotle and all learned clerks
Confirm my reason. Grant that speech is sound
(Because unless it was each word we speak
Would go unheard by any man) and know
That sound is nothing else but broken air;
So speech is air, though loud or soft or foul
Or fair, its substance is just broken air:
And air is broken easily; as fire
Yields smoke by nature, broken air makes sound.
Now air is broken many ways, my friend,
And I'll give two examples: first a flute
And then a harp: blow sharply on a flute
And soon your breath is twisted, broken up;
And pluck a harp-string, hard or soft, the air
Is broken by the stroke and makes a sound:
This is my point; and if a man should speak
He also breaks the air: so now you know.
You'll ask me now, what happens to these sounds,
Of speech and other noises, other sounds:
They multiply, so even the faint squeak
That Mr Mouse makes from his skirting-board
Perpetuates itself and wends its way
To Fame's own House. Now if you still don't think
That this can happen, simply cast your mind
Back down to earth, and think how when a stone
Is cast into the water, first you see
A tiny ripple that soon grows amongst

The other ripples, growing slowly out
All circular and copying themselves
Until the tiny one we started with
Has stretched out to the very banks – you see?
And these brave ripples, though you cannot see
This part, all stretch down *underneath* the lake.
If you do not believe my speech, then try
To prove me wrong! Now just as ripples in
The wounded water stretch out to the bank,
Thus words, that are just sounds, disturb the air,
Though soft or loud, it matters not at all:
The ripples multiply and wander out
Like ripples on a lake, but stretch up high
Instead of wide, and ultimately reach
The House of Fame: this is no joke, though you
May take it thus: it's scientific fact.
Now I must add that speech is a pure sound
That by its very nature must fly up
Into the air – that is its proper home
(I have already mentioned, as you know,
How everything must have its proper place
To which it's drawn by kind; and any speech,
Though foul or fair must fly into the air.)
And so if everything that is must move
Towards that place where it belongs, as I
Have previously stated, so we find
That every sound that finds itself away
From where it feels the most at home must go
By nature and by kind to that same place.
The very place where speech and sound must go
Is home to Fame: her House lives in the midst
As I have said, of heaven, earth and sea;
A place that can conserve both speech and sound.
So to conclude: as I began to say
Some time ago, the speech of every man

That ever was or will be must proceed
To Fame's own House by nature – I am done.
Now tell me truly, have I not set out
The matter here in all simplicity,
Without employing subtle terms or words
Culled from the garden of philosophy
Or poetry, or rhetoric or the tongue
Of baffling philosophers – have I
Not spoken simply, which I know you like,
Preferring it to complicated speech
That tends to overwhelm the simple mind?'
'Oh yes,' I said, 'A ha!' the bird replied;
'It's good to know that I can suit my style
To such an ignoramus as yourself,
And turn the abstract to the concrete so
That he might think he holds it in his hand!
But tell me, did I wind my speech up well?
Did my conclusion seem to follow on?'
'Oh yes,' I said again, 'I am convinced
That what you say is going to prove true.'
'It will be, rest assured,' the eagle said;
'Before this evening you will see laid out
The truth of everything I've said to you.
Your own experience will say to you
That everything is true that I have said:
Your eyes and ears will both attest to it,
That every word of speech that is produced
Ends at the House of Fame, as I have said.'
With this he soared still higher, and remarked,
'The serious stuff is over; now we'll speak
Of lighter things. How are you, little man?'
'I'm well,' I said, 'Oh good,' the bird replied.
'Now cast your eyes down to the land below
And tell me if you recognise a town,
Or house, or any other thing down there

That you have any knowledge of, and I
Will tell you, if you point it out, how far
We are from anything you recognise.'
So I looked down, and saw the plains and fields,
The valleys, forests, rivers and great trees,
And hills and mountains, and the animals
And later, cities; ships upon the sea.
But soon we'd flown so far above the ground
That all the world seemed like a tiny dot,
Or else the thickness of the air between
Shrank it and made it seem so small to me.
The bird spoke up again, 'Now, can you see
Below us anything you recognise?
'I can't,' I said, 'No wonder,' he said then;
'We're higher here than Roman Scipio,
Or Alexander of old Macedon,
Who both saw in their very detailed dreams
Not only hell, but also paradise.
And even Icarus flew lower down;
The son of Daedalus, who flew so high,
The sun's great heat dissolved his waxen wings,
And down he fell and perished in the sea,
At which sight wretched Daedalus was grieved.
Now then, look up,' the eagle said; 'regard
The air that fills this massive space and try
To spot the beasts that Plato once described;
The sky-borne citizens: but do not fear
Their shapes; and also further up you'll see
The galaxy: some call it Watling Street,
While others say it is the Milky Way.
This galaxy was once all scorched with heat
Because a fool called Phaeton, the sun's son
Purloined his father's chariot and rode
Around the sky: the horses quickly knew
The lad could not control them and kicked up

An awful fuss and bucked about the sky
Until he saw the sign of Scorpio.
That frightened him so much, he dropped his reins
And then the horses dragged the fiery car
First up, then down, then up, then down again
Until both air and earth burned grievously,
And Jupiter was forced to kill the boy.
And so we see how wrong it is to let
A fool control a thing that he cannot
Control, because he doesn't have the skill.'
With this, the eagle soared up high again
And still he pleased me with his copious speech;
And while I listened I looked all around
And saw the beasts that dwell in the thin air,
And saw below me tempests, winds and rain,
And snow and hail and mists and also clouds,
And saw how they took form out of the air.
'Oh God,' I said, 'thy power is so great,
And great is thy profound nobility!'
I then thought of Boethius the sage
Who wrote, 'A single philosophic thought
Can fly so high that it can go beyond
The elements, above the very clouds.'
I piped up, saying to the golden bird,
'I know that I am here, but is all this
A dream, or is my body truly here?
You've never told me, and I need to know!'
But then I spoke of Marcian, and then
Of Anticlaudian, and how they both
Described the heavens, and how their own accounts
Both matched what I was seeing, so that now
I could believe them both, 'Oh do shut up!'
The eagle cried, 'you're fantasising now,
When really you should listen to your guide:
Myself, who's ready to describe to you

The stars, unless you say you know them all?'
'Oh no, I can't learn anything,' I said
'About the stars: I fear I am too old.'
'A shame,' the eagle said, 'I'd planned to teach
You all their names and all the star-signs' names,
And where they are: I think that you should learn
Their places in the heavens, because when
You read in poems of how ancient gods
Turned birds or fish or beasts into bright stars,
Such as the Bear or Raven, or the harp
Of Arion, Castor, Pollux, Delphinus,
The Pleiades, or Atlas' seven girls,
You'll know their names, and how they came to be.'
'Please don't,' I cried, 'I just don't need to know
All this, I'll trust the books I have that treat
Of this to keep me in the know; besides
I fear my eyes will not survive the strain
Of gazing at these bodies for too long.'
'You may be right,' the eagle said, and then
Cried out so loud I'd never heard the like:
'Lift up your head, now by St Julian
You'll see a worthy lodging – this is that
Great House of Fame – and can you hear the noise?
That is the sound that rumbles up and down
Fame's House – the sound of news both true and false,
Of speech both kind and bitter, but all loud!
You'll hear no whispers here! But can you hear
That roaring sound?' 'I can,' I said, 'What else
Does that noise sound like?' asked the golden bird,
'The beating of the sea against the rocks,'
I said, 'the hollow rocks, when tempests rage
So loud that you can stand a mile away
And hear the roaring, and the fearful sea
Devours the hapless ships; or it is like
The thunder that will follow a bright bolt

Of lightning cast from Jupiter's own hand:
Whatever it may sound like, I'm afraid
To hear it, and I'm soaked with fearful sweat!'
'Oh, it won't bite you,' said the eagle then,
'It cannot harm you; there's no need to sweat,'
And with that word, we landed near the place:
So near, in fact, that you could cast a spear
From where we landed, and still hit the place.
Somehow, the golden eagle set me down
In a broad street, and told me, 'Take a walk:
With luck, you'll find yourself in Fame's own House.'
'But wait,' I said, 'while you're still here, oh bird,
Please tell me, is this noise, as I have heard
Composed of words all uttered on the earth
That rise up here, as it is said, and is
There not a single being in the house
That stands there, that can make this dreadful noise?'
'By good Saint Clare,' the eagle said, 'you're right:
There is nobody lives there; and what's more
I'll tell you, though it's wonderful to hear,
That when the words arrive in Fame's own House,
As I have told you, they all change themselves
Into the form of those who spoke them first:
That person's clothes (if red or black), his face,
And everything about him is assumed
By his own words, or hers, as I should say,
So you would think the words not his, but him!
Is that not strange,' the eagle said, 'indeed?'
'Oh yes,' I said, 'by God,' and with that word
'Farewell,' the eagle cried: 'I'll leave you here
In hopes that mighty God with help you learn
A thing or two.' I took my leave of him
And walked towards the palace that I saw.

Book III

Oh mighty god of science and of light
Apollo! Lend me some of your great power
To help me finish this last book, the third;
Not that I ever hope to show the world
A shred of mastery in any works
I write; it's rudely fashioned, this I know,
But help me make it readable at least
Despite its limping feet and other flaws,
That come from my disgraceful lack of skill
And ignorance of craft: I simply write
To put across the contents of my head
As simply as I can. Apollo, help
My useless pen to draw the House of Fame.
Now fill up all my heart and give me strength;
And when I chance to spy a laurel tree
I'll kiss it, as I know those trees are yours.
When I had left the eagle, I began
To look around the place he'd brought me to,
And now, without delay, I will describe
The House's shape, its site and the approach
I made to it. It stood upon a rock
So high that it dwarfed all the hills of Spain,
But up I climbed, although the way was hard
And wore me out: I couldn't wait to look

From such a height, and wanted to make out
What type of stone had formed this mighty rock.
It seemed like glass, but glittered more than glass
And what compacted matter it contained
I could not tell at first, from down below.
But when I got up close, I saw the rock
Was one vast block of ice, and not of glass.
'By holy Thomas Becket,' I exclaimed,
'This is a feeble base for such a house
As stands here: surely he that built on this
Should be ashamed, as I hope to be saved!'
And then I saw that one half of the ice
Was all inscribed with famous people's names
Who'd lived in luxury, and were well-known;
But when I tried to read their names, I found
I couldn't: every letter melted off
Before I read it, because fickle Fame
Had turned her back on these once-famous folk:
But then, what lasts forever? you may ask.
I realised that their names had melted off
Because of the sun's heat, and not because
Of dreadful storms that scoured them off at all:
I realised this because I walked around
The hill, and noticed on its northern side
More names of famous people from the past;
But these inscriptions were as fresh and sharp
As if they had been carved that very day,
Or even just an hour before the time
That I discovered them: I saw that they
Had stayed so fresh because of the deep shade
Cast by the mighty tower that loomed above:
This kept them cold, so they could never melt.
I then began to climb the hill and found
On top of it a place the like of which
No man could easily describe at all,

Or ever hope to build so fine a house;
So vast it was, and beautiful to boot.
So wonderfully made was this great house
My mind could hardly take it in at first:
My paltry wit worked hard to comprehend
The beauty of this castle: its rare shape,
The detail of it: I cannot relate
The craftsmanship I saw, but still the place
Is burned into my memory. Its sides
Were formed from precious beryl, tower and walls,
And every room inside, carved in one piece,
Seamless, with curious statuary throughout:
Niches and pinnacles and every sort
Of decoration; windows plentiful
As flakes of snow in winter, and each niche
Cut in the castle's outer walls contained
A statue of a minstrel or a fool,
Such as relate both sad and merry tales
Of people who would like their share of fame.
Among them, Orpheus played on his harp
That sounded sharp and good – and Arion
Another harper, Chiron too who taught
Achilles, and Glascurion the bard
And many other harpers of less note
Who sat about on chairs as students sit
At their professor's feet, and crane their necks
To look up at the master and aspire
To mimic him like apes or 'prentices
Who try to emulate the master's craft;
And standing further down I saw the tribe
Of minstrels in their thousands who inflate
The droning bagpipe or apply the shawm
To their pursed lips, or play on other pipes
Equipped with reeds, or not, while others use
Their mouths to eat at feasts; and there were pipes

And flutes aplenty, even the rude pipes
That little shepherds make out of green corn
And play to soothe their sheep like Tityrus
And Pseustis, shepherds both. Proud Marsyas
Was represented there, who lost his skin
Because he thought that he could beat the god
Apollo as a piper: flayed alive
Was foolish Marsyas; they stripped the hide
From his whole body, face and chin as well.
In that same place I saw a worthy throng
Of Netherlandish pipers, young and old,
Who sing in Dutch, and leap and dance for love.
Nearby in a large space I observed
The noisy martial trumpeters who play
When armies clash and bloodshed stains the field.
Messenus I heard then, the trumpeter
Of Trojan Hector, praised in Virgil's lines,
And also Joab's sound I heard, who blew
His trumpet for King David, and the man
Who blew his trump at Thebes; Thiodamas,
And many other trumpeters I saw
And heard, who'd blown at Aragon in Spain
And also Catalonia: and nearby
Arranged on various seats I saw a host
Of folk with sundry instruments, the like
Of which I'd never seen or heard: they seemed
As numberless as stars, so I will not
Exhaust you with a full account, or waste
Your precious time or mine by setting down
Each tiny thing, because they say that time
Once past, can never be recalled again.
But I saw tricksters there, and jugglers,
Clairvoyants, magic-men and sorcerers;
The makers of strong charms, and exorcists
Who'll fumigate a devil-ridden house;

And I saw masters of all magic arts,
And witches who conspire to change the fate
Of victims, and can make them sick or well,
By studying the stars and wicked books.
Among this jostling crowd I saw the queen
They called Medea; Circe, and the girl
Calypso, who detained on her warm shore
The brave Ulysses. Hermes Belinous
And Elymas and Simon Magus too
I saw there, and I recognised them all:
All these had won their fame by sorcery,
And also Col the juggler who had
A windmill bound up in a walnut-shell.
By why should I name all the folk I saw,
When that might take us to the end of time?
When I had seen them all and found that I
Could wander freely in that curious place
I looked at all the beryl walls and thought
That they shone brighter than the brightest glass,
And also thought that they revealed to me
The qualities of Fame. I saw the gate
Of this fine castle looming on my right
All carved with matchless figures, though I thought
That some were carved by chance, and not by art.
I need not give you many details here
Of all the gate's fine carvings and designs,
Its flourishes and tricks of masonry;
The corbels full of figures that I saw.
I'll only say that it looked very fine,
Not least because it glittered with bright gold.
So through this gate I went, and quickly dreamed
I heard a multitude all crying out,
'Oh lady of this castle, may God keep
Your highness safe; we come here in a throng
To beg a boon of you, for us and ours!'

The multitude that said this was composed
Of hyped-up nobles: some were crowned like kings,
With jewelled crowns and ribbons on their clothes.
And following these, I next saw a great crowd
Of heralds, pursuivants and other types
Who follow after rich folks and are paid
To cry them up: each one of these was dressed
In what we call a coat-armour, and all
These coat-armours were very stiff and rich
With fine embroidery, though every one
Was different: I'm afraid I haven't time
Or space to tell you what diverse designs
Of heraldry I saw on these: I'd need
A bible twenty feet in width for that!
I'll merely say that anyone who knew
Some heraldry would spot upon those coats
The arms of all the famous folk who've lived
In Europe, Africa or Asia since
Both heraldry and chivalry were born.
Really, I'm quite unsure what I should write
To set the scene for you – the very walls
That served as background to this noisy rout
Were plated inches thick with shining gold:
Not common gold, but such as they melt down
To make Venetian ducats – those fine coins
Of which my purse is sadly innocent.
Those golden walls were set as thick as grass
With niches that displayed enough fine stones
To fill a lapidary, or book of gems;
Too many, certainly, to set down all
Their names; and I must speed things up a bit.
This gorgeous hall that I describe was home
To Fame herself, more crowded, I should think
Than any other place. She sat upon
A throne imperial upon a dais,

A ruby throne – composed of that red stone
That sometimes people call a carbuncle;
And there she sat in perpetuity,
A creature unlike anything that lives
In nature. Very small she was, I guess,
A cubit's length, or less, a tiny thing.
But as I watched she seemed to grow in size;
And soon, although her feet still touched the earth,
Her head touched heaven, where the seven stars
All shone around her; but much more than that,
I saw she had as many eyes as birds
Have feathers, or as many staring eyes
Than I have read in John the four fine beasts
Possess, that sit about God's mighty throne.
Fame's hair was curled and wavy, all at once,
And shone like burnished gold: her many ears
Stood up like like asses' ears, and many tongues
Were seen about her person, numerous
As hairs on beasts; and on her feet I swear
She had small wings like partridges', and round
Her neck and all her body glittered gems,
And other precious things. As I observed
This curious titan, all her palace walls
Reverberated to the sound of songs
With heavenly melodies and harmony,
Such as the muses, sisters nine, might sing:
For instance fair Calliope, who seems
So meek in her expression. The great song
I heard about the ruby throne went thus:
'Goddess of renown and fame, praise be!'
When I looked up, I saw the castle's queen
Sustained upon her shoulders the great names
And arms of those whose fame would never die:
The Macedonian conqueror, and he
Who died by a poisoned shirt, brave Hercules

And Alexander: so this goddess sat
In splendour and great riches, but I'll now
Stop talking about her and yank my verse
Onto some other theme. Fame's noble hall
Was home to many pillars that comprised
A noble colonnade that seemed to march
Around the walls, down to the door and back
To Fame's red throne. These gracious pillars shone
With many metals, none as fine as gold,
But all inscribed with noble words, and all
With statues crowning them: now I will say
Who stood on each, beginning with the first,
Who stood upon a pillar made of lead
And also iron, metal of grim Mars;
The saturnine historian of the Jews,
Josephus, Israel's chronicler, who bears
Upon his ample shoulders all the fame
Belonging to the Hebrews: also there
Upon that gold and iron pillar were
Another seven worthies, who all wrote
Of battles and were there to take their share
Of the great weight that old Josephus bore
Upon his Martial pillar, that contained
Not only iron but lead, the metal of
Fell Saturn, who must turn his heavy wheel.
Beyond Josephus was a mighty row
Of pillars bearing other statues which
I will describe, not that I knew them all
Or can recall them all in order, or
Intend to tell you every single one,
Because I fear your patience may be stretched
Beyond endurance, reader. To resume:
I saw an iron pillar that was striped
Just like a tiger's hide, and on it stood
The poet Statius whose *Thebaid*

Holds up the fame of Thebes; whose native town
Was fair Toulouse in France; Achilles too
Was used by this same Statius as a theme.
By Statius stood great Homer, Dares too
Upon an iron pillar; Lollius
Was also there, and Dictys; from Colonne
In France the famous Guido; also there
From Monmouth, Geoffrey: all of these held up
The fame of Troy – a heavy thing to bear!
These worthies who held up the fame of Troy
Did not agree among themselves at all,
And one said Homer lied about the war
And made the Greeks the heroes, which they weren't.
Then I saw Virgil on a pillar formed
Of iron, covered in a coat of tin.
This Roman's task was to support the weight
Of bold Aeneas' fame: right next to him
Was Ovid on a copper pillar; he
Was charged with holding up the fame of her
Whose name his poetry had spread abroad;
Fair Venus, god of love. He stood so high
Upon his pillar, I could barely see
The poet: this fine hall, it seemed to me
Had grown in length and height a thousand fold,
In breadth as well, since I had come inside.
Beyond great Ovid I could see upon
An iron pillar, sternly made, the man
Who wrote about the Romans' civil war:
The poet Marcus Lucan, who sustained
The fame of Julius Caesar, Pompey too
Upon his shoulders. By him stood the clerks
Too numerous to name, who down the years
Have written about Rome and her great works.
Nearby upon a sulphur pillar stood
Another poet, Claudian, who bore

The fame of Pluto, Hell and Proserpine;
The latter, queen of all dark Hades' pains.
But why should I go on like this? The hall
Was full of writers of old tales as oaks
Are full of nests for rooks, and to recount
Each tale and who their authors were would make
A most confusing poem. While I stood
Admiring all this, a great noise approached
That sounded like the noise the bees will make
Before they swarm: a noisy murmuring
It seemed to me, for all the world. I looked
Around and then saw entering the hall
A massive crowd of people from all lands
And folk of all conditions, rich and poor,
Who live beneath the moon. As soon as all
These people gained Fame's presence, they all fell
Down on their knees before this noble queen
And cried out, 'Shining lady, grant us all
A favour, through your grace,' and soon the queen
Had granted some their boon, denied to grant
The wishes of a few, and granted some
The total opposite of what they'd asked.
Now why she did this, I have no idea:
It seemed to me that all these folk deserved
The best of Fame, but some were badly served
By her: it was as if she tried to act
Like Fortune her false sister; anyway
I'll tell you how she served the thronging crowd
Who begged for her good offices and prayed
'Good lady, grant us all a worthy fame:
Our good works in the world have been enough
To give us shining names eternally!'
'By God,' said Fame to them, 'I warn you now,
You'll not get shining names from me at all,
And therefore go your ways, I'll none of you!'

'Alas!' they cried, 'how can you be so harsh?'
'Because I want to be,' said Fame, 'no man
Shall speak well of you in the time to come,
Or ill: your names will vanish on the air.'
And with that word, she called her messenger,
And ordered him to hurry off and fetch
Old Aeolus, the god of wind, or else
Be blinded. 'You will find that god in Thrace,'
Said Fame, 'and when you find him there, make sure
He brings the clarion men call Clear Praise,
Which we employ to herald men's good Fame,
And also Slander, which we like to use
To shame our victims with an evil name.'
The messenger was soon in Thrace, and found
This Aeolus inside the rocky cave
Where he detains the howling, captive winds,
Who roar like bears, they are so tightly bound.
The messenger demanded that the god
Rise up and follow him to Fame's high house
And bring his clarions: this Aeolus
Then ordered one called Triton to convey
The clarions; and raised a fearful wind
That seemed to strip the sky, and carried them
To Fame's high palace, where they soon appeared
By Fame herself, and there they stood like stones.
And soon there came another company
Of virtuous types, who soon began to cry,
'Good lady, if you will, please grant us all
Good fame, and let our noble works shine out
As God will bless you, lady – grant our wish!
I think it's fair to say we've all deserved
Eternal names: good fame is ours by right.
'As I may thrive,' said Fame, 'I will not grant
The greatest of you fame such as you seek.
Today, good works will not assist you – no;

Today, I'll tell you what, I'll give you all
Bad fame and rotten names, though you deserve
Much better, I admit. Now Aeolus
Pick up the trumpet lying at your feet
That men call easy Slander, and blow hard,
So every man will trash these with their tongues,
Instead of praising them, as they deserve:
Make sure you blow the opposite of all
The virtuous things they've done in their good lives!'
'Alas,' I thought, 'what rotten luck for these
Good creatures to be shamed in this foul way,
When everyone can see that they deserve
Good names: but still, there's nothing to be done.'
And so bold Aeolus took up a trump
Of brass as black as hell and blew so hard
I thought the world itself would be blown down.
Through every region of the earth the sound
Resounded, quick as pellet from a gun,
Blown out by powder touched with a hot flame.
The slanderous trumpet belched out clouds of smoke
In nasty colours – deep reds, blues and greens;
Such smoke as one sees curling in the sky
When men are melting lead in a black forge;
But as I watched I noticed that the smoke
Grew larger as it rose into the sky,
Just like a river running from its source;
And that it stank like the foul pit of hell.
So by this process all those folk were wronged
And were condemned for ever to be known
As wrong-doers, though innocent, by all!
There entered then another company,
Who crowded round the dais and quickly fell
Onto their knees and begged the fickle queen
To let them be remembered as they were,
No more nor less, for better or for worse.

The queen replied, 'I deem that you shall have
A lying fame, too good to be the truth,
That puffs up your good works and makes you seem
Far better than you are, although your foes
Would be annoyed to see you fare so well.
Good Aeolus,' she added, 'now put down
Your swarthy trumpet and take up the one
That mean call Praise and blow until their names
Are known throughout the Earth,' she said, 'I will,'
Said he, and set a golden trumpet to
His mouth, and blew it east and west and south
And north, as loud as thunder sounds, and all
The people were amazed to hear the sound.
The smell that came out of the trumpet's mouth
Was like sweet balm and roses both combined.
But now another company appeared:
The fourth, although I saw they were but few.
These also ranged themselves before the throne
And begged the queen, 'Oh lady bright, we here
Have done good all our lives, but are unknown:
Please keep it that way, for in truth we did
Those good things just for gain – not good itself.'
'You have your wish,' said Fame, 'your names are
dead.'
With that, I turned my head around and saw
Another crowd of people who knelt down
To ask the lady to obscure their lives
Because they'd never cared a jot for fame
But only done good works for love of God
And contemplation. 'Are you mad?' asked Fame,
'And did you really think you could do good
And have no Fame? You disrespect me now,
And so I'll see your fame will never end.
Blow Aeolus!' she cried, 'and sound the fame
Of these,' and so the golden trumpet spread

Their fame through all the world, and heaven too.
And then I saw another host come in,
Who also called aloud on Fame, and said
'Great lady, mercy: in our troop you'll find
The people who've done nothing all their lives!
While other folk have worked at this and that
We've all been idle and not tried at all
To leave a mark, or quest for anything.
We've never lifted finger to achieve
A lady's love, for instance, even with
A brooch or ring, or any other gift.
We haven't even tried to win the heart
Of any lady just by being nice,
To get her into bed; so other folk
Assumed that if a woman loved us, she
Must surely be quite mad. We've always tried
To weigh up effort against work, and get
The most of anything that we might want,
Like honour, while we lived in idleness.
Now, with your help, great lady, we would like
To live in fame as worthy, wise and good,
And happy; also fortunate in love,
Although we've won no women in our lives:
Glue women to our names, great Lady Fame!'
'I will comply,' Fame said, 'now Aeolus,'
She added, 'blow on gold and give them all
They asked for: let them all be satisfied.'
And Aeolus again blew loud, and all
The world received the fame of this sixth group.
The seventh company appeared just then,
And all of them fell down upon their knees:
'Great lady Fame,' they cried, 'we beg of you
That you will grant us everything you gave
To that last group,' 'You pigs!' great Fame replied,
'You idle, rotten, lazy, musty swine!

So you want fame, but you won't work for it?
You should be taken out and hanged, you thieves!
You're like a lazy cat, who wants a lunch
Of tasty fish, but guess what? He disdains
To get his claws wet! Curse you, idle fools!
And if I grant your wish, let my own curse
Come down upon my head! Now Aeolus,
Great king of Thrace, make sure you blow these folk
A sorry reputation – do you ask
What you should say? I'll tell you – tell the world
These are the people who would have good fame
But will not work for it, or even do
A shred of good, to earn a shred of fame!
No doubt if they saw beautiful Isolde
They wouldn't fall in love with her, but some
Plain drudge who works at grinding corn would please
Their hearts!" So Aeolus again stood up
And blew through his black trumpet, and the sound
Was loud as all the winds of hell, and full
Of mocking jokes, that chattered like mad apes.
The noise swept round the world, and all the jokes
Made all the people laugh like lunatics.
Another company came after them,
Made up of traitors, vandals, wicked scabs
Whose foul deeds were beyond what normal folk
Could even think of in their darkest dreams.
These villains begged to be remembered well,
As if they'd lived their lives in such a way
That not a drop of scandal would bedew
Their names in future times. 'No way!' said Fame,
'It were a vice, and quite unjust if I
Should grant your wish to be untouched by shame.
I will not do it! There's an end to it!'
The next group leaped into the space and soon
Were thumping everyone they came upon

On their bare heads; and soon the mighty hall
Was echoing the sound of their sharp blows.
'Great lady Fame,' one said, 'we're shrewish folk,
As you will hear: we'll tell you all about
Ourselves: we love all wickedness, just as
Good people love all goodness, and we love
The fact that all the world knows what we are,
So full of vices and of shrewish ways.
And so we beg you not to whitewash us
By ordering a gleaming, golden fame,
But tell it like it is!' 'I grant your wish,'
Said Fame, 'but tell me, who the hell are you,
The spokesman for the shrews? Why do you wear
A fool's stripe on your stockings, and a bell
Upon your cape?' 'I am the one,' replied
The shrew, 'who burned the temple that once stood
In Athens, that was dedicated to
The goddess Isis, truly, that was me.'
'And why did you do that?' asked Fame; 'Because
I wanted to be famous like the men
I saw about the city, whose great names
Were household words to the Athenians.
Their fame sprang from their goodness, but I thought
Bad people can achieve such fame as well,
Although that's of a different stamp, of course.
And so I burned the temple down, because
I knew I'd never be renowned for good,
And so I settled for an evil fame.
So, lady, order Aeolus to blow
Our fame as wisely as you can.' 'I will,'
Said Fame, 'You heard the man! Now blow your
horn!'
'I heard right well,' said Aeolus, 'I'll blow
Their fame so loud that people will believe
My trumpet is the one whose sound will mark

The end of all the world!' With that, he took
His trumpet of black fame and blew and puffed
As he had promised. As I stood and watched
In this great hall I looked around and saw
A man who stood behind me. He began
To speak to me politely. 'Who are you?'
He asked, and, 'Have you come here to find fame?'
'Friend, I have not,' I answered, truthfully,
'The reason I am here, I swear, is not
For that, and, if you will, I'll tell you I
Would sooner die than anyone should have
My name to hand – I know just what I am,
As well as anyone with my small skill,
And what I think, and I do not need Fame
To tell me or the world about myself.'
'Then why have you come here?' the fellow asked.
'I'll tell you,' I replied, 'why I stand here:
To hear new tidings, that is what I want,
To learn, and gather all the happy news
Of love, or anything – that's why I'm here.
The one who brought me here – he promised me
That I would see and hear some wondrous things,
But actually, I haven't yet observed
Or heard the things I really hoped to see.'
'You've not?' he asked, 'I've not,' I said; 'I've known
Since I had wit that there were different types
Of fame, which some desired and some did not;
Although I never knew till now just where
Fame lived or how she looked or how she gave
Her judgements, till I came to this strange place.'
'So what have you *not* seen in Fame's great hall
That you would like to see?' he asked, 'but wait,
I know the answer. Come with me: you'll see
The things you long to see; let's leave this place.'
And so we left the castle, and outside

I saw a valley – in that valley was
A house more strange than Daedalus's maze;
The famous Labyrinth, not so well made
As Fame's great castle, which looked down on it.
This strange house never a knew a second's peace
Or stillness, but it twisted all about,
And never stopped for breath, as houses should.
And it was noisy! If it stood at York,
I'm sure the folks in Rome would easily
Perceive the sound. It sounded like the noise
A giant stone will make as it is thrown
From some great siege-engine or catapult.
The House of Rumour was all made of twigs:
Some yellow, and some red, and others green,
Still others white; the kind of twigs men use
To make up baskets, also panniers.
The noise was all made up of squeaking sounds
And chirpings, and it roared out through the doors
That were so many, they were like the gaps
Between the leaves of summer forest trees:
A thousand, more, to let the sound roar out.
These myriad doors were never closed by day;
They stayed unclosed by night as well, it seems.
There was no need of porters to unlock
The doors to admit the latest piece of news.
The place was always restless, and filled full
Of gossip, scandal, endless whisperings
And louder speech; of marriages, and wars,
And mutterings of peace, and voyages,
Of work, and rest, and death, and life, and love,
And hate, accord, and strife, and victories,
Of health, and sickness, loss, the weather's tricks;
As winds and tempests; also news of plagues
Of men and beasts, and diverse changes in
Estates and regions; tales of jealousy

59

And trust, and wit, and folly, and great fear,
And plenty's smile, and famine's misery,
Of ruin and success, and governments
Well-managed or chaotic, accidents
And fires. This house, I tell you truthfully
Was surely heavy, though it swung about,
Because it measured sixty miles in length,
And though its frame is just a cage of sticks,
It will endure forever, as it is
The mother of all news, as the great sea
Is mother to all wells, and every spring.
'In all my life,' I said, 'I've never seen
A house like this,' and as I stood, amazed
I noticed that my eagle had returned
And now stood perched upon a high-set stone.
I went to him and said, 'I hope you will
Allow me to stay here a little more
By God's good love, and let me look around
At all the wonders that are in this place.
The chances are, I'll learn from what I see,
And profit from my knowledge in some way.'
'By Peter, that is why I'm waiting here,'
The eagle said, 'but one thing I will say:
Unless I help you enter this strange house,
I do not think you'll get inside at all,
Because it whirls about so much; but Jove
Has ordered me to help you in this case,
Because he pities your sad mental state,
(Which you, however, bear with fortitude)
And hopes to bring you to all sorts of sights
Of uncouth things, to solace your hurt heart.
He pities you, and hopes what you learn here
Will heal the heart that Fortune gave to you,
And so he's ordered me to take your part,
And help your cause in any way I can,

And bring you where you'll learn the maximum
That can be learned from such strange sights as these.'
With that, his talons picked me up again,
And put me through a window of the house.
Inside, I thought the house had ceased to move,
And soon I sat upon the floor to watch
The congregation that the house contained.
I've never seen as many people as
I saw inside that place; I had not thought
Nature had made so many – in and out
They roamed, and there was scarce an inch of space
Between their crowded bodies. Every mouth
Was pressed against an ear, and every voice
Was whispering new tidings secretly,
Unless they stood and cried their news aloud.
'You mean to say you haven't heard this news?'
They cried, and, 'No, I haven't; please say on!'
And then the news was told, with many oaths
And promises that it was true, indeed;
'He said that,' 'That he did,' 'These are the facts,'
'I think you'll find it so,' 'I'll dare to say,'
Such phrases whirled around the place, and I
Cannot report them all, why, no man could,
There were so many, thronging in the air;
Some whispered, and some cried aloud. I heard
With some astonishment how every phrase
That passed out of a mouth into an ear
Was soon repeated at another mouth
But with additions, so that every scrap
Of news that did the rounds in that strange place
Increased and snowballed, be it true or false.
The news ballooned, or spread like sudden fire
That starts out as a spark, but soon consumes
A city as it multiplies itself.
The scraps of news that grew inside this place

Flew out the windows when they had increased
Sufficiently to leave the gossips' throng.
Some orts of news did not fly through the doors,
But slyly crept out through a narrow gap
And flew off rapidly. I also saw
Some true news and a lie that both at once
Approached a window but could not go through,
And so each claimed the precedence, but one
Suggested he should go out first, but said
'If I go first, I swear we'll never part:
We'll be sworn brothers, quite inseparable;
And if some angry man should try to split
The two of us, he'll fail: we'll muddle on
Together in men's whispers, or their cries.'
Thus, I saw truth and falsehood fused in one
Confusing and misleading piece of news.
The tidings that escaped the house of sticks
Flew straight to Fame, and she gave each a name,
Depending on her mood, and also gave
Each one a sell-by date, some long, some short,
So that they waxed and waned like the fair moon.
She let them go at last: and wonders flew
In flocks of twenty thousand through the air,
Blown out by Aeolus like rattling shot.
The House of Rumour, both by night and day
Was full of shipmen, pilgrims, couriers,
With bags all stuffed with lies and scraps of news.
Some pardoners were there, and messengers,
With boxes filled with falsehoods to the brim;
And as I roamed about and tried to learn
The nature of this house, and tried to trace
The truth of something I had vaguely heard
About some country there (I will not say
Exactly what it was – there is no need,
And other writers can relate the thing;

The truth will out though soon or late, as sheaves
Of wheat must leave the barn or go to waste);
But as I roamed about I heard a noise
So loud it filled the hall – although it came
From just one corner, which was set aside
For news of love. I turned my head around
And watched the corner, which was quickly filled
With people who ran to it, crying out
'What's that?' and 'I don't know!' The gathering crowd
Was soon so dense that late-comers were forced
To climb onto the backs of those who'd run
The fastest to jam into the small space.
And then they cast their noses up, and eyes,
And trod upon each other's heels, and stamped,
Like people trying to kill migrating eels
That slither through the grass when it is damp.
At last I saw a man I'd never seen
Before, he seemed of great authority . . .

[Left unfinished by Chaucer]

Select Glossary

ACHILLES: Remembered in the *House of Fame* as the Greek hero who gave up his mistress Briseis to Agamemnon during the Trojan War. He is also mentioned as a student of the centaur Chiron.

AENEAS: The hero of Virgil's epic poem the *Aeneid*, completed in 19 BC. Aeneas is a son of King Priam of Troy who escapes the destruction of Troy by the Greeks and wanders about the Mediterranean having adventures until he founds Rome. As a son of Venus, he is favoured by that goddess.

AEOLUS: Keeper of the winds and king of the island of Aeolia.

ALEXANDER: In medieval stories about Alexander the Great, he rides through the air in a chariot drawn by griffins. In *The House of Fame*, he is named as one of the heroes who enjoy enduring fame, whose names and arms are sustained on Fame's shoulders.

ANCHISES: Father of Aeneas, whom the hero rescues from Troy by carrying him on his back. In Chaucer's poem, Anchises also appears to Aeneas when he re-meets dead friends in the underworld.

ANNE or ANNA: Sister of Queen Dido of Carthage.

ANTICLAUDIAN: *The Anticlaudian* or *Anticlaudianus* by the twelfth-century French poet Alain de Lille includes a journey to heaven.

APHRODITE: Greek name for Venus (see below).

APOLLO: Greek and Roman god, son of Jupiter and Leto and brother of Diana. Chaucer invokes him as a god of science and light at the beginning of Book III of *The House of Fame*. Apollo was also a god of prophecy, healing and poetry, among other things.

ARIADNE: Deserted by Theseus, although she helped him kill the minotaur.

ARION: A legendary harper of ancient Greece who was represented in a constellation.

ARISTOTLE: Ancient Greek philosopher who was particularly highly regarded in the Middle Ages. The universe of Chaucer's *House of Fame* is heavily influenced either directly or indirectly by Aristotle's view of the cosmos as described in his *On the Heavens*.

ASCANIUS: Son of Aeneas. Some sources say he was the same as Iuolo (see below).

ATLAS: Titan: husband of Pleione and father of the Pleiades or Seven Sisters – Chaucer mentions the constellation.

BOETHIUS: Roman philosopher (c. 480-524 AD), author of *The Consolations of Philosophy,* which was widely read in the middle ages: Chaucer produced his own English translation of this work.

BRISEIS: A prisoner of war used as a mistress by Achilles (see above) who 'betrayed' her in that he was forced to abandon her to Agamemnon.

CALYPSO: Nymph who detains Ulysses on her island with the use of magic: here she features among other sorcerers and sorceresses.

CASTOR: One of the twins of the constellation Gemini, with Pollux.

CHIRON: Centaur who taught Achilles to play the lyre.

CIPRIS: Another name for Venus or Aphrodite, which references her miraculous birth from the sea near the Mediterranean island of Cyprus.

CIRCE: Sorceress. In Homer's Odyssey, she turned Ulysses' men into pigs.

CLAUDIAN: Called the last Roman poet, Claudian lived from around 370 to 404 AD and wrote descriptions of Hell and its inhabitants in his poem *The Rape of Proserpine,* finished in 397 AD.

COL: An English magician known to have entertained the French in the late fourteenth century.

CROESUS: King of Lydia (now part of Turkey), c. 595-546 BC, famous for his wealth, hence the phrase 'rich as Croesus'. Chaucer is evidently drawing on a version of Croesus' story where he is executed after losing a war because he had misinterpreted a message from an oracle. According to the later Greek historian Herodotus, Croesus survived an attempt to execute him. The oracle had told Croesus that if he made war against the Persians, a mighty empire would fall – this turned out to be Croesus' own empire.

DAEDALUS: Father of Icarus (see below). He also designed the labyrinth for King Minos, which Chaucer compares to his House of Rumour.

DANTE: Dante Alighieri, Italian poet (1265-1321), author of the *Divine Comedy*. A huge influence on Chaucer, who was able to read his works in the original Italian, and mentions him by name in the *House of Fame* and elsewhere. Like the *House of Fame*, the *Divine Comedy* is a poem based on a supposed dream.

DARES (PHRYGIUS): A character in Homer's Iliad who is supposed to have written an account of the war. A book called *Daretis Phrygii de excidio Trojae historia* is supposed to be a Latin translation of this.

DEIANIRA: Inadvertently killed her husband Hercules by smearing his shirt with poison, which she believed to be a love-potion.

DELPHINUS: A dolphin-shaped constellation: the dolphin is supposed to have rescued the harper Arion from pirates (see Arion above).

DEMOPHOON: King of Athens, who deserted his new wife Phillis, a Thracian princess, on his way home from the Trojan war.

DICTYS: The *Dictys Cretensis Ephemeris belli Trojani* is a fourth-century Latin re-telling of the story of the Trojan war, supposedly translated from a Greek original by one Dictys Cretensis.

DIDO: Queen of Carthage, a city in Africa, the later ruins of which can be seen in the modern country of Tunisia. She falls for, sleeps with and is betrayed by the Trojan hero Aeneas, and kills herself.

ELCANOR: Named by Chaucer in the *House of Fame* as a famous dreamer, but scholars are unsure who this person is supposed to be. One theory is that she is Helcana, who appears to her lover in dreams in an old French version of a book called *The Seven Sages of Rome*.

ELIAS: Greek name for the Old Testament prophet Elijah, named here by Chaucer as someone who flew up into heaven, in his case in a fiery chariot (2 Kings: 2).

ELYMAS: A sorcerer mentioned in the New Testament Book of Acts (13:8).

ENOCH: In Genesis, a descendant of Adam who is taken by God, presumably bodily, up into heaven (Genesis 5:24).

GANYMEDE: A Trojan hero, said to be the most

beautiful of all mortals, who is abducted by Jupiter to serve as his cup-beater (Chaucer says 'butler'). In *The House of Fame* he serves as an appropriate example of someone who is abducted and carried up into the air. Jupiter either turned into an eagle to seize Ganymede, or ordered an eagle to do the job.

GEOFFREY OF MONMOUTH: Twelfth-century British historian whose History of the Kings of Britain suggested that the British were originally refugees from the Trojan war.

GLASCURION: May be a reference to the Welsh bard Geraint Fardd Glas (Geraint the Blue Bard) who would have played the harp and may have lived in the ninth century AD.

GUIDO DELLE COLONNE: Thirteenth-century Italian author of a Latin prose history of the Trojan war.
HELICON: Chaucer seems to think this is a well near Parnassus, where the muses live. In fact it is a mountain nearby.

HERCULES: Inadvertently killed by his wife Deianira, who poisoned him by giving him what she believed to be a love-potion. She suspected he loved Iole better than her. Mentioned as one of the heroes whose fame endures because his name and arms are sustained on Fame's shoulders.

HERMES BELINOUS: Belinous is supposed to have discovered a book under a statue of the god Hermes which revealed to him all the secrets of the universe.

HYPSIPYLE: Wife or lover of the hero Jason, whom he deserted and left on her home island of Lemnos.

ICARUS: Son of Daedalus who flew too close to the sun and melted the wax that held together his artificial wings.

IOLE: Loved by Hercules, who at the time was married to Deianira. Deianira tried to win Hercules back with a love-potion that turned out to be poison.

ISAIAH: Old Testament prophet, used here by Chaucer as an example of a famous dreamer. Isaiah has a dream of peace and harmony among the nations (Isaiah 2: 1-5).

ISIS: The spokesman for Chaucer's 'shrews' claims to have burned down the temple of Isis in Athens, just to become famous. The poet may have been thinking of one Herostratus, who burned down the temple of Diana at Ephesus for this reason, possibly in 356 BC. Herostratus is mentioned by the Greek historian Strabo.

IULO: Son of Aeneas. Some sources say he was the same as Ascanius (see above).

JASON: Used as an example of a man who betrayed a woman or women. Jason, for instance, deserted Medea, the mother of his children, whom she then murdered.

JOAB: Jewish military commander mentioned in the Old Testament Second Book of Samuel as blowing a trumpet (see II Sam 2:28).

JOSEPHUS: Jewish historian (c. 37-100 AD), author of *Antiquities of the Jews*, *The Jewish War* and other works. Chaucer probably refers to him as a member of the 'secte saturnyne' because the Jewish religion was associated in the medieval mind with the planet Saturn.

JOVE: King of the gods, also called Jupiter, the Thunderer, and Zeus. Sometimes Chaucer seems to mean the Christian God when he mentions Jove.

JUNO: The wife and also sister of Jove, who holds a grudge against the Trojans and tries to do them harm whenever she can.

LATINUS: In Roman mythology, a king of the Latins who made a treaty with the Trojans.

LAVINIA: Daughter of Latinus (see above). Her father gave her to Aeneas as a wife, which angered Turnus, a local king: this led to war.

LOLLIUS: Named as an author who dealt with the subject-matter of ancient Troy. No such book by a Lollius seems to exist, and it is thought that here and in his *Troilus and Cressida* Chaucer is either making a mistake or deliberately referring to a non-existent source.

LUCAN: Latin poet, 39-65 AD, whose epic poem the *Pharsalia* tells the story of the Roman civil war between Julius Caesar and Pompey.

MARCIAN: Martianus Minneus Felix Capella, a Latin writer of the fifth century AD whose *Marriage of Philology and Mercury* includes a description of the

71

cosmos in Book VIII.

MARSYAS: Satyr who challenged Apollo as a musician, lost and was flayed alive.

MEDEA: In ancient Greek mythology, she was betrayed by Jason, and killed their children. She also appears in the poem among a group of sorcerers.

MERCURY: Messenger of the gods, who tells Aeneas he must leave Dido.

MESSENUS: Trumpeter mentioned in Virgil's *Aeneid* – see Book 3, line 239.

MORPHEUS: Classical god of sleep, described in Ovid's *Metamorphoses*. Here Chaucer gives him a thousand sons, but Ovid suggests Morpheus was himself one of the thousand sons of the god Hypnos.

NABUCO: I have used an Italian version of the name Nebuchadnezzar, the English version of which does not fit easily into a line of blank verse. Nebuchadnezzar, king of Babylon, is a famous dreamer – his dream is interpreted by the Old Testament prophet Daniel (Daniel 2: 31-45).

OENONE: Abandoned first wife of the Trojan hero Paris.

ORPHEUS: Legendary Thracian musician, son of Calliope, muse of epic poetry.

OVID: Latin poet (43 BC-AD 17/18), a contemporary of Virgil and author of the celebrated *Metamorphoses,* among other works. Chaucer follows Ovid's description of the House of Fame in book twelve of the *Metamorphoses*, and also refers to his letter, supposedly written from Dido to Aeneas.

PALINURUS: Aeneas's steersman who is swept overboard and drowned after he falls asleep. The hero later meets him on his trip to the underworld.

PARIS: The Trojan hero deserted his first wife Oenone to pursue Helen of Troy.

PARNASSUS: A Greek mountain supposed to be the home of the nine muses, daughters of Jupiter and goddesses of e.g. epic poetry (Calliope), love poetry (Erato) etc.

PHAEDRA: Sister of Ariadne. Theseus ran off with her and abandoned Ariadne on the island of Naxos. Phaedra later fell for Theseus' step-son Hippolytus, with tragic results.

PHAETON: Son of the sun-god Helios, who stole his father's chariot, with tragic results.

PHARAOH: The Egyptian pharaoh has a prophetic dream which is interpreted by Joseph in Genesis Chapter 41.

PHILLIS: Thracian princess and wife of the Athenian king Demophoon (see above). Phillis hanged herself when Demophoon deserted her.

PLATO: Ancient Greek philosopher, whose ideas about the cosmos (perhaps from his *Timaeus*) influenced

Chaucer's depiction of it in *The House of Fame*. Hetherington, in his *Encyclopaedia of Cosmology* (2014) suggests that Chaucer's cosmos in *The House of Fame* is, whoever, overwhelmingly Aristotelian.

PLEIADES: The constellation of the Seven Sisters, named after their mother Pleione, wife of the titan Atlas.

POLLUX: One of the twins of the constellation Gemini, with Castor.

PSEUSTIS: A musical shepherd in the *Eclogue of Theodulus*, a popular medieval poem attributed to Gottschalk of Orbais, a ninth-century Saxon monk.

SCIPIO: According to Cicero, the Roman general Scipio Aemilianus (185-129 BC) had a dream where he viewed the earth from a great height.

SIMON MAGUS: Sorcerer and controversial convert to Christianity mentioned in the New Testament Book of Acts (8:9-24).

SINON: The archetypal traitor: in Virgil's *Aeneid*, he persuades the Trojans to bring the Trojan Horse into their city.

STATIUS: Roman poet, c. 45-96 AD, who wrote the *Thebaid* about the conquest of Thebes by the sons of Oedipus. He also wrote an unfinished epic about Achilles. Chaucer thinks he came from Toulouse in France, which he did not. Statius's pillar has tiger stripes because some sacred tigers are killed at a crucial point in the *Thebaid*.

SYBIL (OF CUMAE): She helps Aeneas descend into the underworld to visit his dead father and others.

THIODAMAS: A seer mentioned in the *Thebaid* of Statius, a Roman poet of the first century AD. Chaucer seems to have mistakenly got the idea that he blew a trumpet in Statius's epic poem.

THESEUS: Abandoned Ariadne and took off with her sister Phaedra.

TURNUS: King of the Rutuli, who were based a few miles from Rome. Turnus fought and died in a war against Aeneas and his Trojans.

TITYRUS: Musical shepherd in Virgil's *Aeneid*.

ULYSSES: Greek hero of Homer's *Odyssey*, also called Odysseus.

VENUS: In *The House of Fame*, Chaucer calls himself a devotee of Venus as love goddess, whose presence may be said to dominate the entire poem. As mother of Aeneas and friend of the Trojans she also plays an important part in Chaucer's re-telling of parts of the *Aeneid* in *The House of Fame*.

VIRGIL: Latin poet (70-19 BC), older contemporary of Ovid (see above). Author of the epic poem the *Aeneid*, featuring the Trojan prince Aeneas. Virgil is also Dante's guide to hell in the *Inferno*. Chaucer uses Virgil's account of Fame from Book IV of the *Aeneid*.

Select Bibliography

Ackroyd, Peter: *Chaucer*, Vintage, 2004

Bennett: *Chaucer's Book of Fame*, Oxford, 1968

Brewer, Derek: *Chaucer in His Time*, Longman, 1973

Chaucer, Geoffrey: *The Canterbury Tales* ed. W.W. Skeat, Oxford, 1906

Chaucer, Geoffrey: *Complete Works* ed. F.N. Robinson, Oxford, 1974

Chaucer, Geoffrey: *Complete Works* Vol III ed. W.W. Skeat, Oxford, 1900

Chaucer, Geoffrey: *Love Visions*, trans. Brian Stone, Penguin, 1983

Chaucer, Geoffrey: *The Parliament of Fowls* trans. Simon Webb, Langley Press, 2016

Hetherington, Norriss S.: *Encyclopaedia of Cosmology,* Routledge, 2014

Made in United States
North Haven, CT
25 July 2023

39465197R00050